Create Your Own
DREAMCATCHERS

hinkler

Beyond Your Craftiest Dreams

I remember wandering through an open-air market as a teenager and spying a stall full of dreamcatchers dancing in the breeze. The feathers fluttered and floated. The beads clacked against each other. The supple leather wrapped each web-filled hoop in dazzling colours. I chose a rich indigo dreamcatcher, which later hung between my younger brothers' beds. I knew very little of the history of the dreamcatcher, but I was taken with its unique charm.

According to Native American legend, the night air is filled with dreams, both good and bad. Dreamcatchers, also called 'sacred hoops', were weaved by mothers and grandmothers to protect sleeping children by trapping nightmares and allowing only the dreams that would bring comfort and peace to pass through. Any bad dreams caught in the web would burn up in the morning light.

Dreamcatchers remain perhaps the most recognisable symbol of Native American culture. Believed to have originated with the Ojibwa Chippewa people, today's dreamcatchers have been adopted by most tribes. Authentic dreamcatchers are only made by Native American tribes using natural materials – willow branches, sinew, leather, beads and feathers.

Dreamcatchers began as a traditional Native American handicraft, rising to mainstream popularity in souvenir shops and summer camps. There is an undeniable draw to dreamcatchers! Modern versions may not carry the same spiritual symbolism, but the appeal of creating something beautiful made by hand continues. It is, however, important for us to recognise the rich history of the dreamcatcher and respect the Native American culture that birthed this craft.

Contents

Getting Started

Here are the basic dreamcatcher and wall-hanging components you'll need to be familiar with before beginning. By breaking down the design elements, you'll be able to visualise the construction process more easily.

The Hoop

Most dreamcatchers are based on a traditional circle or teardrop shape. You can create your own frame from branches and wire or you can buy metal rings or wooden embroidery hoops to use. But modern designs are not limited to rounded rims! You can experiment with other geometric shapes or more organic alternatives. Found objects, such as horseshoes or driftwood, guarantee a one-of-a-kind wall hanging. Whatever you choose, the 'hoop' of your dreamcatcher sets the tone for the overall style of your piece.

The Web

You'll need some material to fill in your hoop. Cotton thread, yarn, twine or other types of string work well here to make either a traditional web design or something more abstract with a contemporary flair. Another good filler choice for beginners is to use a crocheted doily or piece of lace to stitch into the middle of your hoop.

The Embellishments

Let's really flex those creative muscles! Feathers, beads and leather may be traditional dreamcatcher choices – and gorgeous additions – but why stop there? The sky is the limit when it comes to today's stylised dreamcatchers and wall hangings. Consider bells, fabric, ribbon, trim, felt, botanicals, shells and rope.

Whether you're going for a minimalist design or over-the-top dramatic flair, the embellishments you choose can radically alter your finished hanging. The quantity and length of those embellishments are the two major choices to make. The rule of odds states that people are drawn to odd numbers of elements in a composition, which creates balance, movement and interest. This can apply to wall hangings too! When adding embellishments, stick to odd numbers of your chosen materials – 3 feathers, 5 flowers or 13 shells, for example.

This is also a time to get outside and get inspired by nature. Remember to only gather items that you have permission to collect. Make seasonal dreamcatchers part of your home décor. I picture evergreen boughs and berries mixed with velvet ribbon and jingle bells for the jolliest winter mobile. Perhaps with a few dried orange slices for an added sensory experience.

Head to a craft store and walk the aisles to find your preferred adornments. When I am pulling together materials for a wall hanging, I often get more supplies than I end up using. This gives me the option to be inspired by the actual process: feeling the weight of each hanging embellishment and seeing the twist and turn of each item as I secure it. While I may have a general design in mind, the end result is always unique.

Tools

There are a few essential items to include in your dreamcatcher-and-wall-hanging toolkit. A good pair of scissors are invaluable for cutting thread, fabric, leather and ribbon. A measuring tape lets you accurately measure those materials. An embroidery needle is necessary for stitching and you need pliers to work wire. Glue may be helpful to affix embellishments or paste down fibre ends. A hot glue gun is a crafter's magic wand! – the glue sets in seconds and dries in minutes. Keep a pencil and some paper on hand, as you will want to sketch out ideas when brainstorming.

Planning Your Design

Thinking through your design is always a good idea before you get started! Here are some things you may want to consider when planning your dreamcatchers and wall hangings.

Brainstorming

The very first question you should ask yourself when planning the design of a wall hanging is 'where will it hang?' You need to take into account style, dimensions, location and occasion. Without that information, you may find your time and talent wasted if it doesn't fit or complement the chosen space. You may want to sketch out your intended design before diving in.

HANDY HINT

Please make wise choices when it comes to safely placing dreamcatchers and wall hangings near children. Curious children or pets could become entangled in low-hanging embellishments, or ingest pieces that are not firmly attached, so ensure that your beautiful creations are stable and hung out of reach.

Colour

You don't need an art degree to understand basic colour theory, but learning to use a colour wheel is not complicated and can greatly help guide your colour choices.

Colours adjacent to each other on the colour wheel are analogous. These colour combinations are harmonious and won't overpower a room. You need three to four colour neighbours in analogous designs, with one as your main focus. You can choose warm colours for a happier, more lively feel (reds, oranges, yellows, browns) or cool colours for a calming soothing effect (greens, blues, purples, greys).

Colours on opposite sides of the wheel are complimentary. They produce a bold colour scheme with high contrast and high energy. Complimentary designs tend to be the focal point in a space, just asking to be noticed.

If you choose three colours that are evenly spaced on the colour wheel, you have a triadic design. These contrasting colour combinations may be bold but they are also balanced.

They may not show up on the colour wheel, but don't forget the power of an all neutral palette. Whites, browns, greys and blacks can be used together for some colour contrast or choose just one and create contrast through the texture of your materials. These colours convey elegance and sophistication. Traditional dreamcatchers take their colour cues from nature, so neutrals are an ideal choice.

A playful way of arranging colour is through the traditional rainbow pattern of ROYGBIV – red, orange, yellow, green, blue, indigo, violet. Using a rainbow colour pattern adds the kind of whimsy just right for a child's bedroom.

Another way to considerably alter the look of a dreamcatcher and wall-hanging design is to play with saturation. The difference between vibrant and muted versions of the same colour is dramatic. Changes in saturation apply to the above colour combinations or can be applied in monochromatic design, meaning variations of the same colour. This is perhaps the simplest to pull off, but it does not lack in style. A great example of monochromatic colour usage is ombre where a colour gradually moves from light to dark.

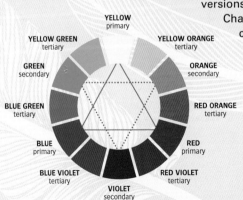

YELLOW
primary

YELLOW GREEN
tertiary

YELLOW ORANGE
tertiary

GREEN
secondary

ORANGE
secondary

BLUE GREEN
tertiary

RED ORANGE
tertiary

BLUE
primary

RED
primary

BLUE VIOLET
tertiary

RED VIOLET
tertiary

VIOLET
secondary

Scale

Scale is as important as colour choice. Bigger does not always mean better, but on the other hand an undersized piece will not have the same impact. Will it be competing for wall space? Will it look dwarfed next to large windows, artwork or furniture? The relationship of the dreamcatcher to the objects it will hang near is important. Smaller rooms tend to require delicate artwork – smaller patterns on a smaller scale. But maybe you are hoping to make a dramatic statement with a larger piece. I personally prefer to err on the side of too big rather than too small. Remember to leave wall-space framing your dreamcatchers and wall hangings to give them the attention that they deserve.

You may find creating multiples of your design makes sense to fill the space. This is especially true if you're creating dreamcatchers for an event rather than for home decoration. Whether for a wedding or a child's birthday party, a collection of wall hangings can serve as a photo-booth backdrop or can extend the theme behind a dessert table.

Materials

Mixed media is a term used to describe art and crafts that combine a variety of materials. Dreamcatchers are definitely part of this family. Mixed media crafting allows you freedom but that can be a bit overwhelming. Focus on one or two main materials – lace, felt, rope, plants, branches, feathers, etc. – for each wall hanging. The additional materials like thread, wire, beads, etc. will fill in the gaps or add pops of interest.

Before You Begin

Here are a few final things to think about before you get started.

Workspace

Remember to carefully consider where you will be crafting. You don't need a large space, but you will want good lighting and a clear surface to work on. Organise your embellishments in separate containers, so you can effortlessly find and reach all of your supplies. Otherwise it will be out of sight, out of mind. Be mindful of little hands and potential choking hazards! By keeping beads and other small items carefully contained, you also protect children who may be drawn to your exciting workspace. If you are including young ones in the project, be sure to choose age appropriate embellishments and ensure that you are there to supervise.

Construction

It is nearly impossible to exactly replicate a dreamcatcher design. Any time you are working with dreamcatchers, there will be differences in how embellishments hang. Don't be discouraged! Patience is necessary and incremental adjustments will likely be needed.

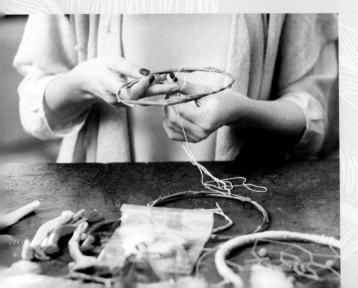

When planning your dreamcatcher design, it helps to visualise the work divided into thirds both vertically and horizontally.

Now place important elements at the intersection of those lines to give balance to your final composition. By choosing one of these composition sweet spots, you provide a focal point. But as is true with most rules, it is fine to break the rule of thirds. Perhaps you will want a symmetrical design, similar to several of the projects outlined in this book. If you have deliberately chosen another focal point, such as colour or an unusual material, you may want to minimise the complexity in other areas of design. Complicated compositions often feel cluttered and disorganised.

Common Knots

There are a few common knots used to attach embellishments and hanging loops to dreamcatchers and wall hangings.

The Overhand knot is the one of the most basic knots we have all been tying since childhood. Form a loop in the cord by passing one tail over the other end. Tuck the tail inside the loop, pull it through completely, and pull taut. (You create a Double Overhand knot by tucking the tail in the loop a second time before pulling taut.)

HANDY HINT

Although much of the wall-hanging construction will take place on a horizontal work surface, you need to plan for some vertical crafting as well. Hold up your dreamcatcher as you attach embellishments to check the suspension of each item.
If you have a larger quantity of embellishments, you may want to secure your dreamcatcher against a wall while attaching them. I have a small peg board in my studio that does the trick when I need to work vertically.

A Reverse Lark's Head knot is used to attach a hanging loop at the top of your piece or to create fringe. Fold the cord in half and lay the folded end on top of the ring. Pass the loop under the ring, bring the tail ends through the loop and pull taut.

A Double Half Hitch knot is attached to a holding cord or other material. You can use this knot to connect cord to your hoop. Beginning with your working cord behind the hoop, wrap the working cord over and around the hoop, forming a counter-clockwise loop with the tail in front, and pull taut. Repeat this process, forming a second counter-clockwise loop to the right of the first half hitch, and pull taut.

Overhand Knot   **Reverse Lark's Head Knot**   **Double Half Hitch Knot**

Basic Crochet Stitches

Slip knot is the first step taken in any crochet project. Create a loop with the yarn, making sure the tail end is dangling behind your loop. Insert the hook through the centre of the loop and hook the tail end, pulling it through and up onto the hook. This is the starting point for the first set of chain stitches.

Chain Stitch (Ch) is the most basic of stitches and begins most projects. Yarn over your hook and draw the yarn through one loop on your hook, leaving you with one loop on your hook. This is the starting point for the next stitch.

Slip Stitch (Sl St) joins stitches to form a ring. Insert your hook under both loops of the chain space you will stitch. Wrap the yarn over your crochet hook, then grab the yarn and draw it through the chain and one loop on your hook, leaving you with one loop on your hook. This is the starting point for the next stitch.

Single Crochet Stitch (Sc) is called Double Crochet Stitch (Dc) in the UK. Insert your hook under both loops of the chain space you will stitch. Wrap the yarn over your crochet hook, then grab the yarn and draw it through the chain. You now have two stitches (or loops) on your hook. Yarn over the hook again and draw through both loops. You now have one loop on your hook, which is the starting point for the next stitch.

Double Crochet Stitch (Dc) is called Treble Stitch (Tr) in the UK. Wrap the yarn over your hook, then insert your hook under both loops of the chain space you will stitch. Wrap the yarn over your crochet hook, then grab the yarn and draw it through the loops. You now have three stitches (or loops) on your hook. Yarn over the hook again and draw through the chain. Yarn over the hook again and draw through two, leaving one on the hook. This is the starting point for the next stitch.

Slip Knot   **Chain Stitch**   **Slip Stitch**

Single Crochet Stitch   **Double Crochet Stitch**

Now you're ready to begin with the projects in this book. Learn new techniques and practise the construction of dreamcatchers and wall hangings as instructed in these pages. I hope you end up as inspired as I am!

Ethereal Feather Mobile

The dance and spin of ethereal feathers is ideal for a three-dimensional dreamcatcher-inspired mobile.
The unique beauty of each dyed feather and the slight shimmer of sparkly twine is a lovely combination.
Add a modern gracefulness to any corner of your home or studio with this oversized statement piece.

YOU WILL NEED:

- 19 white feathers
- Non-toxic all-purpose coral dye
- Gold hoop (20cm / 8in diameter)
- Spool of gold and white baker's twine
- 19 natural wooden beads (1.3cm / 0.5in)
- Scissors
- Measuring tape
- Hot glue gun

1. Prepare your feathers before starting. Make sure to protect your work area with newspaper or paper towels to prevent staining. Follow the instructions of your chosen dye. Let dry completely.

HANDY HINT

I experimented with different lengths of dye time before settling on a quick 10 second dip covering about 1/3-1/2 of the feather. I recommend having extra feathers on hand for your own dip-dye learning curve.

1.

2.

3.

2. Choose your favourite 19 prepared feathers and arrange for your mobile, working from smallest (at the end of the first string) to the largest (last string). Trim the quills to about 2.5cm (1in). Cut 30cm (12in) of twine for your first feather. Apply a small line of glue on the quill and place the twine on it, leaving an 8cm (3in) tail. Before the glue is set, slip your wooden bead over the tail and quill to cover the join.

3. Once the glue is set, tie the twine above the bead in a Double Overhand knot (see page 6).

4. Repeat this process with each feather, increasing the length of twine by 5cm (2in) for each subsequent feather. Attach feathers to the metal hoop with a Double Overhand knot, which will create a spiral pattern of feather placement.

5. Cut two 76cm (30in) lengths of twine. Wrap them across the hoop to create a symmetrical cross, perpendicular along the diameter of the hoop, looping them around the metal hoop twice for stability. Gather the four ends together and tie in a Double Overhand knot. Once the ends are tied, adjust the hanging loop they make so the mobile hangs level.

HANDY HINT
Hanging a mobile is tricky! It wants to tip and tilt in all directions. I chose to loop the twine around the hoop rather than tie it in order to have more control with adjusting the level. I also find a second pair of hands extremely useful – an obliging assistant can help hold the mobile while you fine-tune this final step.

HANDY HINT
You can change the scale of this design in several ways – the size of the metal hoop, the number of feathers or the hanging-length of each feather. By shortening the gaps between the feathers, you will achieve a tighter spiral if you have limited space to display it.

5.

4.

5A.

Green-Catcher

While I won't promise this wall hanging will help with a good night's sleep, the addition of plants to a space is sure to brighten your day dreams! This piece combines a traditional weaving pattern with a green pop of the unexpected. If you're not comfortable using live air plants, substitute quality faux air plants for a similar look.

YOU WILL NEED:

- Metal hoop (30cm / 12in diameter)
- 8 strand cotton thread in mustard yellow (4m / 4.4yd length)
- 10 air plants of various sizes
- Measuring tape
- Embroidery needle
- Hot glue gun
- Scissors

1. Prior to starting on your hoop, give the air plants a water bath and let fully dry. Make sure to remove any damaged or dead leaves.

HANDY HINT
The key to a green thumb is knowledge! Learn about the care for your specific plants and your specific region to keep them happy and healthy.

2. Start by tying your cotton thread to the hoop. It is helpful to secure the knot with a bit of glue to prevent it from sliding while weaving.

1.

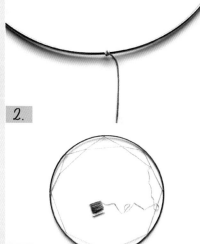

2.

3.

4.

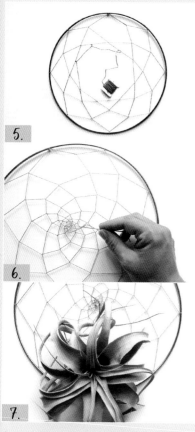

5.

6.

7.

4. Now continue the same looping technique on the strings rather than the hoop, weaving in smaller and smaller circles. Make sure to centre your loops on each string as you go.

5. Then continue, centring each loop until you reach the middle.

6. You will find an embroidery needle useful in the tighter weaving. Tie off the thread when you reach the hoop centre (or when you can no longer fit the needle in the next opening).

7. Place seven air plants in the weaving at the bottom traveling up the right side of the ring. It is easiest to begin with your largest plants first. Place three air plants on the top left side of the ring. Ensure they're placed securely in the web, but ensure that they can easily be removed for water baths.

3. Begin weaving your thread around the hoop. Moving clockwise, pass the thread under the ring. Bring it back over the top of the ring to the left, coming back down behind the loop and pulling taut. (You are not tying these, just simply looping the thread over.) Repeat 7 more times, with the seventh loop at your glued knot. Each loop of these base strings will be about 12cm (4.75in) apart.

Floral Drama

Black and white with a hint of blush, this wall hanging is less sugar and more spice. I can easily picture this as party décor, hanging in my tween daughter's bedroom or anywhere I want to add some boho floral drama.

YOU WILL NEED:

- Wooden embroidery hoop (20.3cm / 8in diameter)
- Black 6mm cotton cord (16.5m / 18yd)
- Faux flowers (I used four types)
- Faux greenery
- Scissors
- Hot glue gun
- Wire cutters

1. Separate your embroidery-hoop pieces and set aside the outer hoop. Glue one end of a 5m (5.5yd) length of rope to the inner hoop. Begin wrapping until all of the wooden hoop is covered.

2. Cut nine lengths of rope to 127cm (50in) in length. Mount each cord to the hoop with a Reverse Lark's Head knot (see page 7).

3. Repeat with remaining cords.

1.

2.

3.

4.

5.

6.

HANDY HINT
I chose these gorgeous white anemones as the main focus of my floral arrangement because I knew the black centres would work oh-so-well with the black rope. The dark (nearly black) purple thistles were another contribution to the moody colour scheme but they are balanced with the pale blush chrysanthemums. The bright green fern gave the arrangement a modern playfulness. And I made sure to respect the rule of odds (see page 3 for more information)!

4. Plan out floral arrangement using the outer hoop as a template. Snip the stems as needed.

5. Begin gluing the flowers and greenery on top of the cords. I found it helpful to picture the floral arrangement in layers. The background layer, which usually contains greenery and the heavier florals, is attached first. The middle layer consists of most of the visual weight. The top layer finishes off the arrangement by covering any unsightly glued stems and filling in gaps.

6. Trim rope fringe at the bottom of the dreamcatcher.

HANDY HINT
You can trim the rope fringe while the piece is laying flat or while hanging on a wall. Scissors work in both cases, but if you have a cutting mat and rotary cutter, you can make short work of this task!

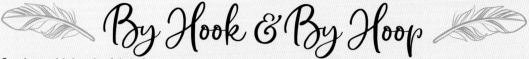

By Hook & By Hoop

Crochet, with its airy fabric formed by interlocking hook and thread, is an ideal filler for a dreamcatcher hoop. Easy to learn, yet highly satisfying, you will create a delightful wall hanging that unites these two traditional handcrafts. Transform the humblest of materials into art!

YOU WILL NEED:

- Hoop (18.5cm / 7.2in)
- White ribbon (2.8m / 112in)
- Hot glue gun or craft glue
- White thread (30m / 32.8yd)
- Crochet hook (4mm / G/6)
- White twine (284.5cm / 112in)
- 10 white feathers
- 10 geometric beads
- 8 oval beads
- 24 small pearl beads
- Scissors
- Measuring tape

1. Begin by covering your hoop with ribbon. First use a small amount of hot glue to secure one end of the ribbon to the hoop. Snugly wrap the ribbon around the hoop with a slight overlap, completely covering it. When you have covered the whole hoop, trim the ribbon as needed and secure the end with hot glue.

2. Crochet your web using the thread and hook. The following rounds are layers of the doily, beginning in the centre and moving out. Round 1: Begin with a slip knot. Ch 4, Sl St to connect ends. 1 Dc, Ch1 into centre. Repeat 7 times (8 total). Sl St in first Dc to connect. Weave in the beginning tail end.

1.

2.

3.

4.

14

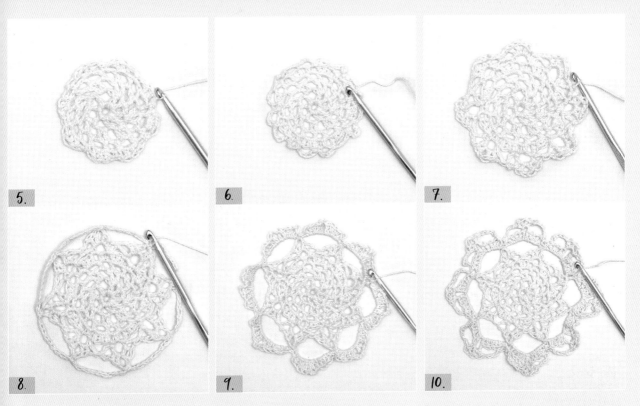

5.

6.

7.

8.

9.

10.

3. Round 2: Ch 3, 1 Dc, Ch 1 in first space. 2 Dc, Ch 1 in seven remaining spaces (8 total clusters). Sl St in Ch 3 to connect.

4. Round 3: Ch 3, 1 Dc, Ch 1 in first space. 1 Dc, Ch 1 in fifteen remaining spaces (16 total). Sl St in Ch 3 to connect.

5. Round 4: Ch 2, 2 Dc, Ch 1 in first space, then 1 Sc, Ch1 in next space. Repeat 3 Dc, Ch 1, then 1 Sc, Ch 1 pattern in remaining spaces (8 total Dc clusters). Sl St in Ch 2 to connect.

6. Round 5: Ch 5, Skip first Dc space, 1 Sc in second Dc space. Ch 5, 1 Sc in next space. Repeat this pattern over each of the seven remaining Dc clusters.

7. Round 6: Ch 2, 1 Sc, Ch 2 into first Ch 5 space. 2 Dc, Ch 2, 2 Dc, in second Ch 5 space. Repeat this pattern around.

8. Round 7: Sl St up to first Dc cluster. Sc in Ch 2 space between clusters. Ch 10, 1 Sc to next Ch 2 space. Repeat this pattern around.

9. Round 8: 1 Sc, 5 Dc, Ch 3, 5 Dc, 1 Sc, Ch 1 in first Ch 10 space. Repeat this pattern around.

10. Round 9: 1 Sc in first Sc space. Ch 6. 2 Dc, Ch 1, 2 Dc in Ch 3 space. Ch 6. Repeat this pattern around.

11.

11. Round 10: 1 Sc, 3 Dc, Ch 1, 3 Dc, 1 Sc in Ch 6 space, then Ch 2, 3 Dc, Ch 2 in Ch 1 space. Repeat this pattern around. Sl St in first Sc to end. Tie off thread and weave in tail.

HANDY HINT

I recommend blocking your doily before attaching it to the hoop. Blocking introduces moisture to finish your crochet by shaping and sizing it, uncurling edges and generally spiffing it up. I just ironed my doily with a light spray of water.

12.

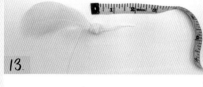

13.

15.

17.

12. Using eight 15cm (6in) lengths of thread, attach the doily to the hoop with single knots. This allows you to centre the doily as you gradually tighten and double knot the pieces of thread. Weave ends into the back of the doily.

13. Cut the following lengths of twine: three 20cm (8in), two 30.5cm (12in), two 40cm (16in). Apply a small line of glue on a feather quill and place the twine on it, leaving a 5cm (2in) tail. Before the glue is set, slip your geometric bead over the tail and quill to cover the join. Tie the ends of the twine together over the top of the bead. Repeat for the remaining six lengths of twine.

14. For the 20cm (8in) lengths, add three pearl beads and one oval bead to each, securing with a single knot. For the 30.5cm (12in) lengths, measure 5cm (2in) from the top of the geometric bead, tie a single knot, add one oval and three pearl beads, and secure the beads with a single knot. For the 40cm (16in) lengths, measure 9cm (3.5in), tie a single knot, add three pearl beads and one oval bead, and secure the beads with a single knot. You now have seven feather-bead embellishments.

HANDY HINT

In most of my craft projects, flat lays of the unassembled components (or laying them out) are my best friend. I find these dry-fits extremely helpful to visualise my end goal, plus I stay more organised and can easily see if I am missing anything.

15. For the middle feather-bead trio, cut a 50cm (20in) length of twine. Slip a geometric bead over the tail. Apply a small line of glue on a feather quill and slip the bead over it at about the 15cm (6in) mark. Repeat for the remaining two beads and feathers, leaving approximately 1cm (0.5in) between the beads. Tie the tail over the top of each bead, ending with the first one you added. This gathers the feathers together. Measure 12.7cm (5in) from the top of the trio, line up with one of the short 20cm (8in) embellishments from step 4 and tie the lengths of twine together.

16. The feather-bead embellishments will hang in the following order, left to right: 20cm (8in), 30.5cm (12in), 40cm (16in), 20cm (8in) with attached trio, 40cm (16in), 30.5cm (12in), 20cm (8in). First attach the 20cm (8in) with attached trio embellishment in the centre, spacing the remaining embellishments 2.5cm (1in) apart. The top of the oval beads should meet the bottom of the hoop for each embellishment.

17. Cut a 30.5cm (12in) length of twine for the hanging loop. Slip the twine under and around at the very top centre of the hoop. Slip one oval bead and three pearl beads through both tails. Knot over the beads and once again at the ends of the tails, creating a 5cm (2in) loop.

Rainbow Unicorn

Are you in need of a mega dose of happy? A rainbow unicorn dreamcatcher may do the trick! For both the young and the young-at-heart, this project is rich in colour, texture and the magic of childhood nostalgia.

YOU WILL NEED:

- Styrofoam wreath (25cm / 9.8in diameter)
- Fleece fabric strip in white (4.6m / 5yd length, 7.6cm / 3in width)
- Styrofoam cone (15.2cm / 6in length, 7cm / 2.75in width)
- Black felt 25x50mm (1x2in)
- White felt 380x455mm (15x18in)
- Pink/peach felt 75x100mm (3x4in)
- Gold sequin thread (11m / 12yd length)
- Felt flowers and leaves
- Felt pom-poms (57 in assorted colours)
- White cotton thread (5m / 5.5yd length)
- Embroidery needle
- Scissors
- Hot glue gun

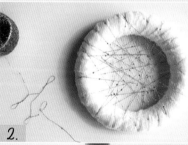

1. Secure one end of the fleece fabric strip to the styrofoam wreath with glue. Once it is set, wrap the fabric around to cover the foam. Secure the end with glue.

2. Tie the gold sequin thread to the wreath and begin wrapping across the hoop at different angles, creating an abstract starburst design. Tie the other end to the wreath when you've reached desired coverage.

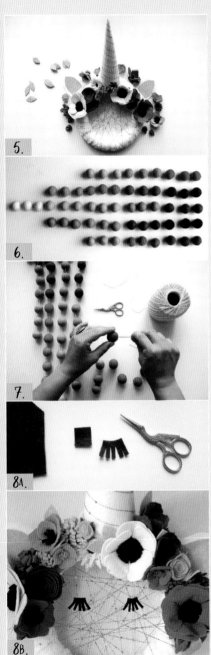

5.

6.

7.

8A.

8B.

3. Wrap the cone in white felt to create a horn. Imagine wrapping a cone shaped present – trim, fold and glue to the form as you would if you were working with paper. Embellish with the gold sequin thread in a spiral pattern. Secure to wreath with glue.

4. Cut out 7.6cm (3in) tall ears from white felt, adding a smaller piece of pink/peach felt to the middle. Secure to the wreath on either side of the horn with glue.

5. Arrange flowers in a design following the colours of the rainbow (see colour wheel on page 4 for assistance) and attach with glue to the wreath form. Vary sizes and styles for interest.

6. Arrange the colourful pom-poms in a rainbow pattern, with deeper colours at the top and less saturated colours near the bottom. The outer columns have 9 pom-poms, the inner columns have 12 pom-poms and the centre column has 15 pom-poms.

7. Thread pom-poms onto white cotton thread with an embroidery needle starting from the bottom of each column. Allow 2.5cm (1in) spacing between pom-poms. Attach by tying the end of the thread to wreath, spacing them 3.2cm (1.25in) apart. Secure knot with glue.

8. Make eyelashes by cutting two 25mm (1in) squares from black felt. Next make four small snips on one side and gently spread apart. Decide on placement, then add small dots of glue to the gold webbing and attach eyelashes gently.

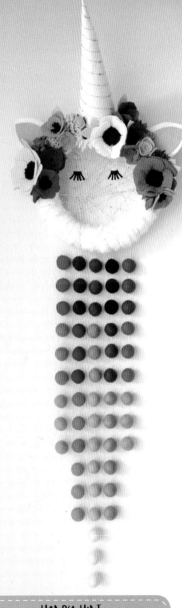

HANDY HINT
Store-bought felt flowers are available locally and/or online. Consider making your own felt flowers for ultimate control on colours and varieties.

Beach Dreaming

If your inner mermaid dreams of the sea, hang a sweet beach memento even if you are land-locked. Made with natural elements in a non-traditional shape, this wall hanging could be made with either found or store-bought materials.

YOU WILL NEED:

- 5 pieces of driftwood (12cm / 5in)
- 18 pieces of turquoise sea glass
- Twine (2.75m / 3yd) divided into thirds
- 18-gauge aluminium wire (3-5m / 5-6yd length)
- Hot-glue gun
- Wire cutters

1. Begin by cleaning your materials thoroughly, especially if they were collected rather than purchased. When fully dry, you will want to lay out your design elements, making decisions on which order to place your driftwood and sea glass. Space the branches and sea glass out with 2.5cm (1in) gaps.

2. Add a small amount of hot glue to the centre of the top piece of driftwood and, leaving about 25cm (10in) free at the top, hold the twine on it until set. Hold up your hanging after adding each branch to test the level and spacing.

3. Next, wrap the twine around the branch twice to the right and twice to left of the glued section. Secure with more glue when finished. Repeat with the other pieces of twine on either end of the branch.

4. Next you will wrap each piece of sea glass in wire. Cut 18 pieces of wire 20-30cm (10-12in) long (length depends on size of the sea glass). Place the centre of the wire length on the front of the glass and twist the tails fully around. Wrap the tails around each other twice. Repeat for each piece of glass.

5. Add your wire-wrapped sea glass to the twine by twisting the remaining tails to the ends of the twine according to your layout in step 1.

HANDY HINT
It is difficult to adjust the sea glass on the twine once it has been wrapped so take your time with this process to get the spacing just right.

6. Snip excess wire. Make sure to tuck in the cut ends to avoid cutting your hands or scratching the walls.

7. Tie a double knot in the twine at the last piece of sea glass, to keep twine from slipping through the wire. Cut excess twine.

8. Back at the top of the hanging, cut the middle piece of twine and glue down. Gather the extra length on the left and right ends and tie together to make your hanging loop.

4A.

4B.

5.

6.

7.

8.

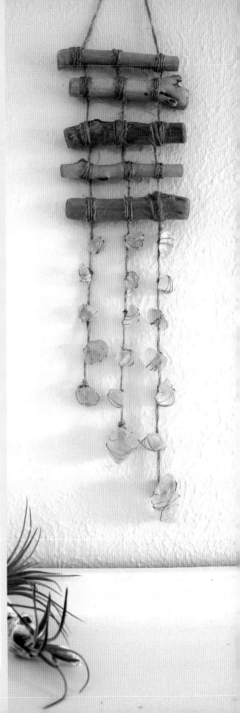

Lace & Found

This is the ideal project to dive into the world of wall hangings.
Delicate lace is balanced by rustic branches. Just a few added
embellishments keep this dreamcatcher simple and sweet.

YOU WILL NEED:

- Four branches (30.5cm / 12in length)
- Piece of lace (15.25x15.25cm / 6x6in)
- Lace ribbon (8.2m / 9yd length)
- Spool of 5ply cotton thread
- 9 white tassels (10cm / 4in length)
- 63 dark wood beads (various sizes)
- Scissors
- Measuring tape
- Embroidery needle (optional)
- Hot glue gun (optional)

1. Begin by cleaning your branches thoroughly. When fully dry, arrange them in a diamond shape and begin constructing the frame. Tie the first corner together with a piece of thread approximately 91.5cm (36in) long. Knot the thread to the bottom branch and then wrap around the intersection until secure. Tie in a simple Double Overhand knot (see page 6) when finished and trim the excess thread. Repeat with the other three corners.

HANDY HINT
The frame will have some movement, but if there is still too much wiggle in the joints, a small of amount of glue at each intersection will be helpful to steady it.

1.

2.

3.

4.

2. Tie the thread to each corner of the piece of lace. Then attach your lace square to the frame by tying the lace corners to the corners of the frame using four lengths of thread, 61cm (24in) long. Trim the excess threads after tying the Double Overhand knots to secure the lace.

HANDY HINT
Depending on the intricacy of your lace pattern, you may find an embroidery needle necessary for attaching the thread. I was able to slip the thread into a larger opening in the lace corners without the aid of a needle.

3. Attach 183cm (72in) lengths of thread to the top of each tassel and fold over to make 92cm / 36in hanging loops. Mine had thread, but I made it longer to match these lengths. Add seven beads to each hanging loop in the pattern of your choice.

4. Gather the tassels into groups of three, arrange them in a staggered pattern and tie the tops of the hanging loops together creating a final group length of 81cm (32in). By tying the tassels together and treating them as one element, you limit the number of items you mount on the hoop which simplifies the design.

5. Tie your embellishments to the bottom three corners using Reverse Lark's Head knots (see page 7). Then place a 182cm (72in) length of lace

ribbon behind each set of tassels and a second piece of lace ribbon measuring 101cm (40in) in front of each set of tassels. Tie all to the diamond, ensuring the ends are staggered. You may need to adjust the knots or trim the ribbon tails to create a pleasing composition.

6. Add a hanging loop for your wall hanging by using a 38cm (15in) length of ribbon. Wrap it under the top corner and tie the ends together.

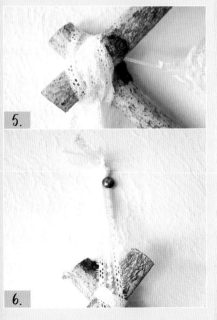

5.

6.

Congratulations!

You have crafted stunning dreamcatchers and wall hangings! Are they hanging in your own space or have you given them as gifts to brighten someone else's walls? Regardless, I have a feeling there are fresh ideas brewing for your next creation.

I love the current trend of dreamcatchers used as event décor. They bring the dreamiest boho vibes to a garden soiree. On a larger scale, they create a stunning statement backdrop, especially when grouped in multiples. And miniature dreamcatchers make sweet sentimental party favours. Consider incorporating your newfound dreamcatcher skills in the planning of that next special occasion.

Making dreamcatchers is a lovely choice for a group activity. Grab your best mates and have each bring an embellishment to share for a delightful crafternoon. It is such a gift to create in company.

Do you have leftover materials from a previous crafty endeavour? Dreamcatchers and wall hangings are easily customisable and they provide a great opportunity to use up any leftover craft supplies you may have. Be eco-friendly and use up the remainder on a one-of-a-kind creation. Did you collect shells, leaves or driftwood during a recent trip? You can use these to create a special travel memento dreamcatcher or wall hanging.

Here's the secret behind making your own dreamcatchers and wall hangings: You can't mess these up. These dreamy creations can fit any aesthetic and ability. Remember to enjoy the process. Happy crafting!

Meet the Author

Hey there! My name is Annalea Hart – wife, mama, fibre artist, plant lover and chai drinker. My husband Jesse and I live in picturesque Albuquerque, New Mexico, raising and homeschooling five wonderfully exhausting children. My days are primarily filled with the world-changing work of motherhood, but I also find pockets of time for my favourite creative pursuits. I believe all of us are meant to be creative! ROPE & ROOT, our family business, combines a love for hand-crafted macramé with the natural beauty of botanicals. Whether it's living room walls, commercial installations or stage design, I've had incredible opportunities to turn humble materials into something much more than the sum of their parts. Teaching others to do the same is my favourite thing! I love serving our community, investing in my city and dreaming of ways to be radically generous. When we're not adventuring outdoors, our family specialises in dance parties and pizza movie-nights.